IT'S MY STATE!

MONTANA

Ruth Bjorklund

Ellen H. Todras

Cavendish
Square

New York

Published in 2014 by Cavendish Square Publishing, LLC
303 Park Avenue South, Suite 1247, New York, NY 10010

Library of Congress Cataloging-in-Publication Data

Bjorklund, Ruth.
        Montana / Ruth Bjorklund, Ellen H. Todras.
                p. cm. — (It's my state!)
        Summary: Surveys the history, geography, government, economy, and people of Montana — Provided by publisher.
        Includes bibliographical references and index.
        ISBN 978-0-7614-7999-4 (hardcover) — ISBN 978-1-62712-100-2 (paperback) — ISBN 978-0-7614-8006-8 (ebook)
        1. Montana—Juvenile literature. I. Todras, Ellen H., 1947- II. Title.
        F731.3.B54 2013
        978.6—dc23   2012026679

This edition developed for Cavendish Square Publishing by RJF Publishing LLC (www.RJFpublishing.com)
Series Designer, Second Edition: Tammy West/Westgraphix LLC
Editor, Second Edition: Emily Dolbear

MONTANA

CONTENTS

State Flower: Bitterroot

Bitterroot is a small, low-growing pink wildflower. Its scientific name is *Lewisia rediviva*, in honor of American explorer Meriwether Lewis, who collected the plant in Montana in 1806. The root of the plant was important in the diet of American Indians, who considered it a valuable trade item. The Flathead and Shoshone Indians mixed the root of the bitterroot with berries and meat.

State Bird: Western Meadowlark

The western meadowlark is a brightly colored black and yellow songbird that lives in meadows and perches on fence posts throughout the state. It eats seeds, grains, caterpillars, cutworms, grasshoppers, and other insects. This bird builds a nest of grass and bark on the ground, woven into the surrounding plants.

State Tree: Ponderosa Pine

The most widely distributed tree in the western United States, the ponderosa pine got its name because it is so large and heavy, or ponderous. The ponderosa pine reaches heights of 100 to 150 feet (30 to 45 meters).

State Animal: Grizzly Bear

Grizzlies range in color from blond to dark brown and black. Their humped shoulders are used to power their forelimbs in digging. Grizzlies are omnivores, which means that they eat both plants and animals. Depending on their age, gender, and available food, grizzlies weigh from 200 to 800 pounds (90 to 360 kilograms). Despite their size, they can run up to 35 miles (56 kilometers) per hour.

State Fish: Black-spotted Cutthroat Trout

The black-spotted cutthroat trout has black spots that run down its back and pinkish-red streaks under its jaw. This fish is a favorite food of grizzly bears.

State Fossil: *Maiasaura*

The duck-billed dinosaur *Maiasaura* lived about 100 million to 65 million years ago. The name *Maiasaura* means "good mother lizard" in Greek. *Maiasaura* fossil finds provided the first evidence that dinosaurs cared for their young, much as birds do now. Adult *Maiasaura* weighed about 6,000 pounds (2,800 kg). *Maiasaura* probably traveled in herds. Their fossilized eggs and bones have been discovered in Montana at a large bone bed called Egg Mountain.

The Treasure State

Montanan A. B. Guthrie Jr., author of the 1947 Western novel *The Big Sky*, once remarked, "I've always thought of Montana as my center of the universe." With a land area of 145,546 square miles (376,962 square kilometers), Montana is the fourth-largest state in the nation. Montana is as large as or larger than such countries as Germany, Ecuador, and New Zealand. The state is divided into fifty-six counties.

Montana's landscape is varied. The eastern part of the state has high plains, long winding rivers, badlands, and isolated mountain ranges. In the west are the rugged Rocky Mountains, scenic valleys, canyons, fast-flowing rivers, alpine lakes, forests, waterfalls, and snow-white glaciers. Above it all is a dramatic view of wide, open sky, earning the state the nickname "Big Sky Country." Montana's more common nickname, however, is the Treasure State because, at one time, it produced so much of the country's gold, silver, and copper.

Great Plains

The central and eastern sections of Montana, which make up two-thirds of the state, belong to the region of the United States called the Great Plains.

Quick Facts

MONTANA BORDERS

North	Canada
South	Wyoming
	Idaho
East	North Dakota
	South Dakota
West	Idaho

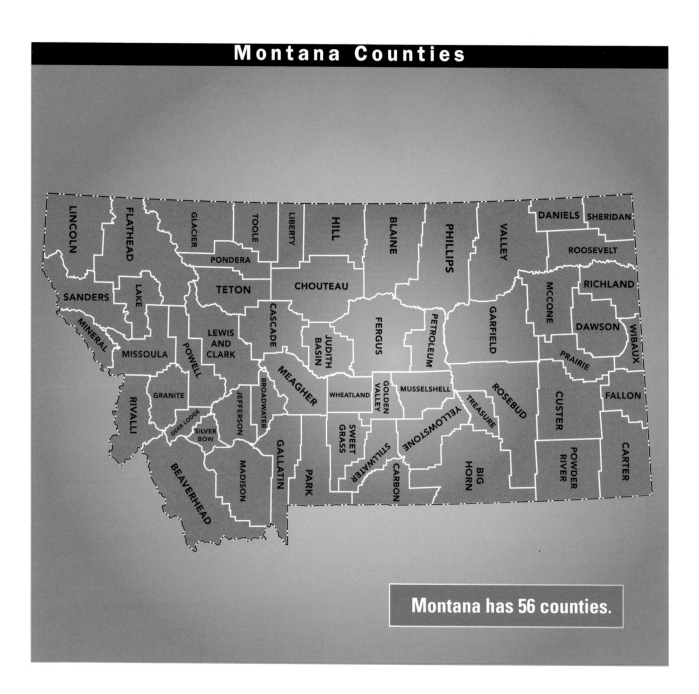

Montana has 56 counties.

In parts of Montana, grasslands grow just as they did thousands of years ago.

At first glance, the area appears flat and perhaps unremarkable, but the plains are bursting with natural history. For most of the past 8,000 to 10,000 years, native grasses such as buffalo grass, blue grama, and blue bunch wheatgrass covered the plains and fed huge herds of bison. By 1900, however, most of the bison had been killed and farmers began to replace much of the grasslands with planted rows of crops.

During the last Ice Age, which ended about 11,000 years ago, huge sheets of slow-moving ice called glaciers advanced and receded. As they moved, they carved rugged mountain crest lines, scraped valleys flat, and left behind rocks and debris. As the ice melted, river valleys, potholes, lakes, and wetlands formed. Today, these areas provide rich habitats for red monkey grass and wild asparagus, as well as wild turkeys and ring-necked pheasants.

Central and eastern Montana's two major rivers are the Missouri and the Yellowstone. The Missouri River has its source in southwestern Montana, near Three Forks. It carves a sweeping route north along the foothills of the Rocky Mountains and then flows eastward through the plains. In north-central Montana, at Great Falls, the river drops 500 feet (150 m) in a series of rapids and waterfalls. Farther east, a 149-mile (240-km) stretch of the river has been designated by the U.S. government as the Upper Missouri Wild and Scenic River. This portion of the river flows through spectacular scenery, in an area little touched since American explorers Meriwether Lewis and William Clark visited the region in 1805 and 1806. In this area, called the Missouri Breaks, the river races eastward past rock cliffs, sandstone towers, and ash, juniper, and cottonwood forests.

East of the Breaks, the Fort Peck Dam transforms the Missouri River into a series of long lakes. Fort Peck Lake is one of the largest human-created lakes, or reservoirs, in the United States. It is 134 miles (216 km) long and 220 feet (67 m) deep. Surrounding the reservoir is the Charles M. Russell National

In the spring, the landscape of western Montana near the Rocky Mountains features rolling green hills.

A train carrying grain passes by the Missouri River in western Montana.

Wildlife Refuge. This refuge is home to ducks, mule deer, pronghorns, elk, bighorn sheep, white-tailed deer, grouse, eagles, and migrating birds.

The Yellowstone River is the longest undammed river in the United States, excluding Alaska. It begins high in the mountains of northern Wyoming and flows into Montana. The river is a total of 671 miles (1,080 km) long. It stretches 570 miles (917 km) through Montana. *National Geographic* magazine called it "the last best river."

Quick Facts

YELLOWSTONE RIVER

Near Billings, Montana, the Yellowstone River flows past high, yellow bluffs. A local Indian tribe, the Minnetaree, called the river *Mi tsi a-da-zi* ("Yellow Rock River"). Early French adventurers called it *Roche Jaune*, which means "yellow rock." English-speaking explorers later named the river Yellow Stone.

The Yellowstone is filled with fish such as cutthroat trout, grayling, and paddlefish. Its banks are lined with cottonwood, poplar, and willow forests that provide a habitat for creatures such as bald eagles, red foxes, beavers, otters, and deer. Before white settlement, large elk and bison herds roamed the plains near the Yellowstone River. When Lewis and Clark traveled through the area in 1805, they observed many herds of bison crossing the river.

Hundreds of millions of years ago, eastern Montana's plains lay at the bottom of a shallow sea. The land collected rich organic material called sediment. As the sea dried, the sediment turned to rock. Buried in this rock are dinosaur bones, seashells, and other fossils. Water and wind have worn down the rock in many places, leaving dramatic land formations often called badlands. About 80 million years ago, magma surged up from deep within Earth. Magma is extremely hot liquid rock that is called lava once it reaches the surface. As the lava cooled and hardened, it formed mountain ranges in central and eastern Montana. Rising sharply from the flat prairie, these mountains are eye-catching walls of rock with scattered forests of juniper, western larch, and Douglas fir.

The Rocky Mountains

Montana comes from the Spanish word *montaña* for "mountain." The state could not have a better name to describe its western portion. Some 70 to 90 million years ago, a major disturbance occurred deep within Earth, thrusting rock upward. Volcanoes, glaciers, earthquakes, and other forces of nature went on to shape the mountain chain called the Rocky Mountains.

There are dozens of mountain ranges in Montana's Rocky Mountain region. The state's highest peak—Granite Peak, 12,799 feet (3,901 m) high—rises in the Beartooth Range. Other major ranges are the Anaconda, Bitterroot, Gallatin,

Bridger, Madison, Mission, Swan, and Whitefish, as well as the Centennial Mountains.

Montana is also home to seven national forests. These forests have stands of Douglas fir, ponderosa pine, larch, and western hemlock. Wide valleys wind along the base of the mountains. In these valleys, cottonwoods, juniper, white pine, and western cedar grow against a bright backdrop of blue sky.

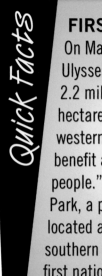

Quick Facts

FIRST NATIONAL PARK
On March 1, 1872, President Ulysses S. Grant set aside 2.2 million acres (890,000 hectares) of wilderness in the western United States for "the benefit and enjoyment of the people." Yellowstone National Park, a portion of which is located along part of Montana's southern border, was the country's first national park.

The Beartooth Range is part of the Absaroka-Beartooth Wilderness. It is home to Granite Peak, Montana's highest point.

The crest of the Rocky Mountains creates what is called the Continental, or Great, Divide. This imaginary line runs north-south through the country. East of the Continental Divide, rivers flow toward the Atlantic Ocean and the Gulf of Mexico. West of the Divide, rivers flow toward the Pacific Ocean.

One region in northern Montana is called the Triple Divide. There, water coming down from different mountain peaks heads toward three oceans. Besides flowing east toward the Atlantic and west toward the Pacific, water in this region also drains down off the peaks into Canada and flows northeast to Hudson Bay and into the Arctic Ocean.

Other major rivers in Montana include the Kootenai, Flathead, Blackfoot, Bitterroot, and Clark Fork. All of these rivers eventually flow into the Pacific Ocean by way of the Columbia River. Most of the rivers have dams that create human-made lakes. Western Montana has many natural mountain lakes as well. Flathead Lake, the largest natural lake in Montana, is also the largest natural freshwater lake west of the Mississippi River. This lake is 27 miles (43 km) long and 16 miles (26 km) at its greatest width, with a maximum depth of 371 feet (113 m).

One lake was actually formed by a naturally created dam. In 1959, a giant earthquake shook loose a wall of rock from a canyon and dammed up the Madison River, creating Earthquake Lake. Today, ospreys and bald eagles make their home in nearby trees and compete with sport fishers for so-called Quake Lake trout and whitefish.

Montana's bodies of water also include dazzling waterfalls. As high mountain rivers race down to valleys, crashing walls of water create special habitats for wild trout and river otters. The black swift, a bird that builds its nest behind waterfalls and lays only one egg each year, can also be found near many of

Montana's waterfalls. Some well-known waterfalls are Palisades, Skalkaho, Natural Bridge, and Kootenai Falls.

Climate

There is nothing dull about the weather in Big Sky Country. In any given year, Montanans can experience snow, hail, drought, floods, thunderstorms, Arctic winds, and desert-hot temperatures. The coldest temperature ever recorded in Montana was –70 degrees Fahrenheit (–57 degrees Celsius) at Rogers Pass, north of Helena, in 1954. This is also the record cold temperature for all of the United States except Alaska.

Frosty temperatures do not last all winter. Instead, they come in two or three waves of cold spells each year. The average winter temperature around the state is about 10 °F (–12 °C). Surprisingly warm winds called Chinook winds often blow in from the Pacific Ocean. These winds melt snow and take the edge off winter's chill.

The Weeping Wall in Glacier National Park is a waterfall fed by snow melting from the mountains.

The warmest temperature ever recorded in Montana was 117 °F (47 °C). This occurred at Glendive in 1893 and at Medicine Lake in 1937. In general, summer brings high temperatures, especially in eastern Montana. Summer days can often top 100 °F (38 °C). But the average summer temperature is 87 °F (31 °C), and cool winds keep most everyone comfortable.

Throughout the year, the pattern of precipitation is consistent. Clouds filled with moisture from the Pacific move eastward. When they hit the Rocky Mountains, the clouds release their moisture in the form of rain or snow. Once

Whitefish Mountain, near Glacier National Park in Montana, gets an average of 300 inches (762 centimeters) of snow a year.

clouds make it over the Rockies into eastern Montana, they have lost much of their moisture.

Although the Glacier National Park weather station records an astounding 120 inches (305 cm) of precipitation each year, the average annual precipitation in western Montana is about 20 inches (51 cm) of rain or melted snow. In eastern Montana, the average is much less, about 13 inches (33 cm). Droughts with only 6 to 9 inches (15 to 23 cm) of precipitation a year are not unusual. While hundreds of inches of snow can pile up in the Rocky Mountain region, fierce Arctic winds blow so hard across eastern Montana that snow seldom stays long on the ground.

Natural Disasters

Earthquakes, slow moving glaciers, storms, and powerful winds helped shape much of Montana's natural beauty, such as mountains, forests, and rivers. These forces of nature have also contributed to the state's severe weather events and other natural disasters. On Montana's Great Plains, warm, moist winds from the Gulf of Mexico flow north while icy Arctic winds travel south. When these two different winds collide, thunder and lightning storms explode overhead. Tornadoes sometimes form. Along with violent winds, these storms carry heavy rains that can cause rivers to overflow, flooding homes and farms.

A summer thunderstorm rolls over the Great Plains of Montana. These conditions sometimes result in tornadoes.

When they are started by lightning, forest fires and grassland brush fires are a part of the natural ecology. (Dry conditions can help feed any kind of fire.) Large animals such as elk or bear can outrun a fire. Small animals such as prairie dogs or chipmunks seek shelter underground. A burned area is a rich hunting ground for owls and other birds looking for prey. Douglas fir trees have thick bark to protect them from burning. Aspens and cottonwoods have deep roots that quickly sprout new growth after a fire. Lodgepole pines grow a type of cone that will open and let loose its seeds only during extreme heat.

Wildlife

Badgers, coyotes, mule deer, and pronghorns live in eastern Montana. The many lakes, ponds, and wetlands are home to a great variety of fish and amphibians. Trout, perch, bullheads, channel catfish, and paddlefish are just some of the fish swimming through the waters. These bodies of water are important refuges for rare migrating shore birds such as the American white pelican and the great blue heron. Eagles, hawks, wild turkeys, pheasants, grouse, and ducks also live near these watering holes.

Eagles, hawks, and other predators depend on the prairie dog to survive. When Lewis and Clark reached the Montana plains, they noted numerous prairie-dog "towns." They were charmed by the animal they called the "barking squirrel." But the farmers considered them pests for building mounds and tunnels through

BOB MARSHALL WILDERNESS AREA

Quick Facts

National wilderness areas are wild places where nature is left untouched by humans. The largest national wilderness in Montana is the Bob Marshall Wilderness Area. It is named after an American environmentalist who in 1935 cofounded the Wilderness Society, an organization that works to protect wild places. Located in northwestern Montana, the Bob Marshall Wilderness straddles the Continental Divide. Montanans fondly call this special place "The Bob."

farm fields. Ranchers noticed that they disturbed the grasslands where cattle fed. As a result, farmers and ranchers killed off nearly all the prairie dogs. Owls, eagles, and ferrets, creatures that relied on prairie dogs for food, also suffered. To protect the region's prairie dogs, the Montana Department of Agriculture has developed a management plan to balance the survival of these animals with the concerns of farmers and ranchers.

Montanans are proud to say that their state has more animals than people. In the forested mountains and the river valleys of western Montana are mule deer, mountain lions, bobcats, woodpeckers, bats, hawks, and black bears. Bison live in the National Bison Range Wildlife Refuge. Different types of snakes and lizards can be found throughout the region.

Some of the nation's rarest and most endangered species live in Montana. When a species (a type of animal or plant) is endangered, so few are left that the species is at risk of becoming extinct, or completely dying out. Endangered species in Montana include the black-footed ferret, the whooping crane, the least tern, the pallid sturgeon, and the white sturgeon.

There are also a number of threatened species in Montana. A species is considered threatened when its numbers are reduced and it is at risk of becoming endangered. Montana has four threatened animal species—the grizzly bear, Canada lynx, piping plover, and bull trout. It also has three threatened types of plants—the water Howellia, Ute lady's tresses, and Spalding's campion.

Some animals that almost vanished have begun to come back. Many of these populations decreased because of overhunting, loss of habitat, or pollution.

Bison live in the National Bison Range Wildlife Refuge in Montana. They also migrate north to Montana from Yellowstone National Park during the winter months.

Laws now prevent fishers from harming various fish species. Similarly, other animal species, including peregrine falcon, bald eagle, gray wolf, and Rocky Mountain bighorn sheep populations, are being monitored in the state.

North America's heaviest bird, the trumpeter swan, was nearly driven to extinction in the 1930s to provide feathers for women's hats. At one point, there were fewer than two hundred birds, but today, Red Rock Lakes National Wildlife Refuge has thousands. Montanans are proud of their state and want to preserve both its beauty and its creatures. As one Nez Perce elder explained, "I belong to the land out of which I came. The Earth is my mother."

Some animal species, such as the Rocky Mountain bighorn sheep, are slowly increasing their numbers in Montana's secluded wilderness areas.

Beaver

Adapted to living in water as well as on land, the beaver uses its teeth to cut down trees to dam streams, forming ponds that are a rich habitat for fish, birds, deer, and other creatures throughout Montana. Beavers also build cone-shaped houses called lodges. Beaver lodges are built in ponds. They are sturdy enough to withstand bear attacks and usually have two escape tunnels for emergencies.

Common Camas

Early American Indian groups valued the common camas so much that the people would battle over ownership of camas fields. This blue-flowered, onion-like plant was harvested for its bulbous roots. The roasted roots taste like sweet potatoes. Gatherers need to be careful because the poisonous white camas often grows near common camas.

Dusky Grouse

The dusky grouse lives in western Montana. In the winter, this bird lives in stands of evergreen trees at high elevations. In the summer months, it moves to the edges of forests at lower elevations. The dusky grouse has a long, square tail and ranges between 2 and 3 pounds (0.9 and 1.4 kg) in weight.

Canada Lynx

The Canada lynx has a thick coat, tufts of fur on its ears, and a short black-tipped tail. A threatened species, the lynx lives in the remote pine and fir forests of Glacier National Park. A nighttime hunter, the lynx excels at catching rabbits in the snow because its large, furry paws act like snowshoes.

Paddlefish

Paddlefish have lived in Montana's rivers for more than 300 million years. This large fish is shaped like a shark, but with a long paddle-shaped snout. The paddlefish uses its snout as a feeler and eats as some whales do—by filtering water. Though the paddlefish eats only tiny animals called zooplankton, it can grow up to 6 feet (2 m) long and weigh up to 120 pounds (54 kg).

Rubber Boa

The rubber boa hunts at night and likes cool weather. This snake gets its name because its loose skin feels like rubber. It catches and then kills its prey by constricting—or squeezing—the small animal to death. Scientists have noticed that the tails of many rubber boas are scarred from adult mice attacking them while the boas eat their favorite meal of baby mice.

From the Beginning

Through prosperous and poor times, and glory and sorrow, the people of the Treasure State have struggled and survived. Former U.S. senator Mike Mansfield once said of his home state, "The history of Montana is the song of a people who . . . have held together, persevered and, at last, taken enduring root."

The First People

The first people who lived in today's Montana were early American Indians, now known as Paleo-Indians. They are believed to have been descendants of people who crossed a land bridge that once connected Asia and North America more than 10,000 years ago. Over time, they moved south along what is now known as the Rocky Mountains. The route that they (and many later groups of Indians) followed is now referred to as the Great North Trail or the Old North Trail.

Archaeologists (scientists who study past cultures) have found evidence that there was human life in what is now Montana at least 7,000 years ago—and perhaps much earlier than that. These prehistoric people hunted animals such as woolly mammoths and ancient bison. They also gathered plants for food. In time, the climate became very hot and dry, and the mammoths and bison moved on. This forced the Paleo-Indians to seek out smaller animals and to rely more on plants growing in river valleys.

In the 1890s, students of all ages learned at this one-room schoolhouse in the mining town of Hecla. It is now a ghost town with only a few deserted buildings.

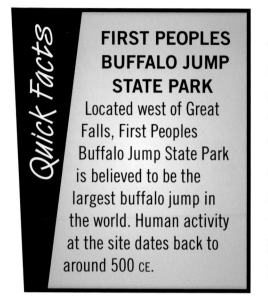

About 2,000 years ago, the region's climate became cooler, and bison herds flourished again. American Indian descendants of the Paleo-Indians followed the herds and made good use of the bison. They used all of the animal for food, clothing, tools, fuel, and material for making their homes. These hunters caught their prey by driving the bison herds off of high cliffs, known as buffalo jumps. The Indians called these buffalo jumps *pishkun*.

In other areas, people have found tepee rings, which are the remains of early dwellings. American Indians in the region lived in portable tents called tepees, which were made of bison skins and log poles. To keep the tepees fixed to the ground, the Indians held the bison skins down with circular piles of rocks, known as tepee rings.

Historians estimate that Shoshone and Blackfeet Indians have been in what is now Montana since at least 1600. The Shoshone came from the south. They were the first people in the area to breed, ride, and trade horses. Their horses were acquired from other Indian groups who got them from Spanish explorers in the American Southwest during the late 16th century.

Other tribes that settled along the west side of the Rocky Mountains were the Kootenai, Kalispel, Salish, and Bannock. On the plains, the Crow settled along the Yellowstone River. The Gros Ventres, Assiniboine, and Cheyenne tribes later followed.

The men of the Plains tribes hunted mostly bison. The American Indians of the mountains and western valleys hunted deer, trapped small animals, and fished. The women prepared and preserved the meat. They also treated the animal hides for clothing, accessories, and home building. Women of the Plains tribes gathered berries, such as huckleberries, and dug roots, such as wild carrot, onion, turnip, common camas, and bitterroot.

Buffalo jumps, or *pishkun,* are an ancient method of hunting bison by driving them off cliffs. Today, people can find spear points, animal skulls and horns, and other prehistoric artifacts if they dig near a buffalo jump.

MAKING A MODEL TEPEE

A Plains Indian tepee was perfectly suited to nomadic life. Nomads moved from place to place looking for food, water, and grazing land for their animals. A tepee was easy to transport and kept cool in the summer and warm in the winter. By following these instructions, you can make a model tepee.

WHAT YOU NEED

Brown paper grocery bag

Sponge

Water

Piece of plain paper, $8\frac{1}{2}$ by 11 inches (22 by 28 cm)

Scissors

Crayons in a variety of colors

4 thin round sticks (such as barbecue skewers), about 6 inches (15 cm) long

One 6-inch (15-cm) piece of string or raffia

Clear tape

Ruler

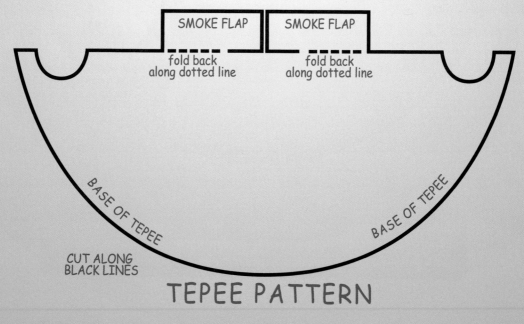

SMOKE FLAP   SMOKE FLAP

fold back along dotted line   fold back along dotted line

BASE OF TEPEE   BASE OF TEPEE

CUT ALONG BLACK LINES

TEPEE PATTERN

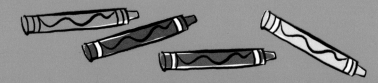

Cut the bottom off of the paper bag. Lay the paper flat and wipe both sides of the paper with the damp sponge. Crumple the paper to make wrinkles. Lay the paper in the sun or by a window to dry. This technique makes the paper look like tanned leather.

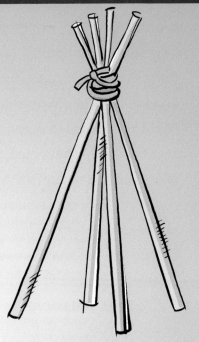

Using the template given here, trace the tepee pattern on the plain paper. Cut out the pattern.

When the brown paper can be handled without tearing, place your pattern on the brown paper. Trace the pattern onto the brown paper and then cut it out. While the cutout is still flat, use crayons to draw traditional designs such as arrows, suns, horses, bison, geometric patterns, circles, and lightning bolts.

Take the four sticks and use the string or raffia to tie them together about $1\frac{1}{2}$ inches (4 cm) from the top, spreading out the opposite ends. The sticks should form an upside-down cone.

Wrap the brown paper tepee cutout around the sticks. (The circular edge of the cutout lies along the wide end of the cone.) Tape the brown paper to the sticks on the inside. Fold the two smoke flaps back.

You can cut out a small circle from the leftover brown paper. This will be your winter door cover for the opening at the front of the tepee. If you like, make a few more tepees and arrange them together to create an Indian village.

Exploration

Even though American Indians and their ancestors had been living on the land for thousands of years, rulers in Europe claimed the region during the eighteenth century. In 1743, two French-Canadian brothers, François and Louis-Joseph Vérendrye, were probably the first Europeans to visit the region that includes present-day Montana. Both men worked as fur trappers. They were also explorers and looking for a river route to the Pacific Ocean. They did not find the river route and returned home. Although many decades passed without Europeans setting foot in the region, France claimed the land as its own. Present-day Montana was part of an area that the French called the Louisiana Territory.

In 1803, France sold the Louisiana Territory to the United States. The acquired territory included more than 800,000 square miles (2,000,000 sq km) of land west of the Mississippi River. The deal, called the Louisiana Purchase, doubled the size of the United States.

Thomas Jefferson, the third U.S. president, had already planned on sending an expedition to explore the region. He had asked his personal secretary, Meriwether Lewis, to lead a mission. Lewis in turn asked his army friend, William Clark, to join him. The expedition's four goals were to study the Missouri River, find a water route from the eastern United States to the Pacific Ocean, meet native peoples, and gather information about plants, animals, landforms, and climate. The two explorers hired a crew, collected supplies, and began to paddle up the Missouri in 1804.

Lewis and Clark spent their first winter in what is now North Dakota, where they invited a French trapper and his Shoshone wife, Sacagawea, to accompany them on their journey west. Sacagawea often served as an interpreter between Lewis and Clark and the American Indians farther west. Setting out in the early spring of 1805, the group reached present-day Montana in April. Gazing into the valleys between the Missouri and Yellowstone rivers, Lewis wrote that he had a "most pleasing view of the country."

Lewis and Clark and their crew—named the Corps of Discovery—faced many challenges in the area. There was no water route through the Rocky Mountains.

The Lewis and Clark Expedition traveled through Montana on its way to the Pacific Ocean. All but one member of the group survived.

But traveling overland, they managed to cross the rugged Continental Divide, and they reached the Pacific in November 1805. They wintered near present-day Astoria, Oregon.

On their return trip in 1806, the group split up for a time to explore more of the region. They were amazed by the mountains, rivers, trees, plains, valleys, plants, and wildlife. Some of the animals they saw included beavers, bison, deer, elk, grizzly bears, and "vast assemblages [groups] of wolves."

At this time in Europe and in the United States, a fashion craze for men's beaver-felt hats was in full swing. On learning that the territory Lewis and Clark had seen was overflowing with beaver, fur trappers began to trickle into the area. In 1807, Manuel Lisa, a Louisiana Spaniard, was the first to set up a trading post in present-day Montana. He established his post near the Bighorn and Yellowstone rivers.

For the next forty years, riverboats, trappers, and traders from fur companies in the East came to the area. American frontiersmen such as Jim Bridger, Jedediah Smith, Kit Carson, and James Beckwourth rose to prominence in the fur business. These so-called mountain men explored much of the West, including present-day Montana.

Fur trappers used metal traps to catch beavers and stretchers to dry the pelts.

Many of the trappers were Roman Catholics from French Canada. They brought with them some Iroquois Indians from the East, to teach trapping skills to the Indians farther west. While working with the Flathead Indians, the Iroquois told them about the Catholic priests who taught about God and life after death. They called the priests the Black Robes, after their dark-colored religious garments.

Intrigued with these ideas, the Flatheads sent four different groups to St. Louis, Missouri, between 1831 and 1839 to find someone to serve as their priest. The first three groups failed to find anyone, but the fourth was successful. A young Belgian Jesuit named Father Pierre-Jean de Smet agreed to travel back west with the Flatheads. In 1840, he performed a Catholic Mass for the Flatheads in Green River, Wyoming. Then, in 1841, de Smet set up a religious establishment called St. Mary's Mission in the Bitterroot Valley, near present-day Stevensville, where he taught members of the Flathead tribe how to farm. St. Mary's Mission is believed to be the first permanent white settlement in present-day Montana. Later missionaries built and ran a sawmill and a flour mill there.

Wagons West

By the time demand for beaver-felt hats had decreased in the 1840s, most of the beaver population in the region had been wiped out. Many trappers found another line of work—leading wagon trains of pioneers west. Farmers from states east of the Mississippi River had heard tales of the rich, unpopulated land and wanted some for themselves.

Beginning in the early 1840s and continuing for some forty years, hundreds of thousands of families embarked on a four- to six-month journey of about 2,000 miles (3,200 km) to establish themselves on land in the West. The Oregon Trail, which began in Missouri and ended in what was then called the Oregon Country of the Pacific Northwest, was one of the first great pioneer trails.

Soon, however, other trails broke off from the Oregon Trail, for pioneers heading to California and what is now Utah and Colorado. The first major overland route through Montana was called the Mullan Road. This wagon road was named after John Mullan. He was a U.S. Army lieutenant commanded to link Fort Benton on the upper Missouri River with Fort Walla Walla on the Columbia River in today's eastern Washington. This route was completed in 1860. Additional routes through Montana included the Bozeman Trail, which opened in 1864. This trail branched off from the Oregon Trail in present-day Wyoming. The Mullan Road, Bozeman Trail, and other routes were used by miners who flooded into the region after gold was discovered, as well as by settlers seeking land to farm. The U.S. government built army forts along the trails to aid and protect travelers using them.

Gold!

In 1858, near Deer Lodge, Montana, two brothers named James and Granville Stuart discovered gold in a creek bed. Over the next few years, gold was found in Grasshopper Creek near Bannack, at Alder Gulch by Virginia City, and at Last Chance Gulch, now the state capital, Helena. Once gold was found, thousands of miners flocked to the area, with traders, merchants, farmers, and others close at their heels. They quickly turned the remote camps into booming western towns.

When a gold camp was established, there was no federal or state government to impose order. The rough-and-tumble ways of many residents made early mining towns in Montana very dangerous. The wild ways of these towns led to a call for order. Many people wanted Montana to become a U.S. territory, a region that was not a state but had a separate government. U.S. leaders viewed this idea favorably, to a large extent because the Civil War (1861–1865) was taking place at the time.

War and Territory

During the Civil War, the Northern states—known as the Union—fought against eleven Southern states, called the Confederacy. The Southern states had left the Union, largely over the issue of slavery. The two sides fought many battles, and hundreds of thousands of people were killed during this bloody war. Although the conflict took place thousands of miles away, Montana played a role in the war. The Union wanted Montana's gold to help pay for soldiers and supplies.

Montana was part of the Idaho Territory at the beginning of the war. An Idaho official, Sidney Edgerton, saw the need for stronger government in the mining towns. In 1863, he traveled to Washington, D.C., to lobby for territorial status. The Idaho Territory was divided in two, and Montana became a new U.S. territory on May 26, 1864. Edgerton was appointed the first governor of the Montana Territory.

Indian Removal

As settlers and miners moved westward, American Indians were forced off their traditional lands. Many American Indian groups had to sign agreements, or treaties, with the U.S. government. These treaties granted whites the right to settle on or pass through American Indian land, while American Indians increasingly were restricted to living on reservations that included only a small portion of their traditional lands. The Blackfeet Indians did not accept the treaties and often fought bitterly against the U.S. government and white settlers. In the beginning, the Crow Indians agreed to treaties and did not often fight with the new arrivals.

As more and more whites arrived in the west, treaties were broken to make room for the new settlers. Eventually, most American Indian rights to the land were taken away. In 1876, Sioux and Northern Cheyenne Indian leaders including Sitting Bull, Crazy Horse, Gall, and Lame Deer joined forces. Many Indians left their reservations and waged a series of battles with U.S. Army troops sent to capture or kill them.

On June 25, 1876, Lieutenant Colonel George Armstrong Custer and about 200 soldiers set out to attack a Sioux and Cheyenne encampment near the Little Bighorn River in Montana. More than 2,000 American Indian fighters surrounded Custer's band of men. Custer and all his men were killed during the Battle of the Little Bighorn.

The Battle of the Little Bighorn, also known as Custer's Last Stand, took place in the Montana Territory in 1876.

LITTLE BIGHORN BATTLEFIELD NATIONAL MONUMENT

South of Billings lies the Little Bighorn Battlefield National Monument. It memorializes the people involved on both sides of the conflict. In addition to watching an orientation video, visitors can learn from National Park Service rangers about the battle and, during the summer, take walking tours of the battlefield and the Custer National Cemetery.

After the Battle of the Little Bighorn, the U.S. government sought revenge. Congress increased the size of the army and allowed more forts to be built in the region. Large numbers of troops tracked the hostiles, as the resisting Indians were called, and either killed them or forced them onto the reservations. The year 1878 saw the last significant American Indian resistance in Montana.

Railroads and Ranches

In the mid-1800s, rough overland trails and riverboats were the only forms of transportation that linked the Montana Territory with the rest of the country. As the territory grew, it needed better methods of transportation. In 1881, the Utah & Northern-Union Pacific Railroad built a line to Butte. In doing so, it captured the profitable mining trade in Butte. In 1883, the Northern Pacific Railroad laid tracks that connected the northern part of the territory to Portland, Oregon, and to Chicago, Illinois, and other eastern cities. The U.S. government granted land to the railroads to encourage them to build lines through the western frontier.

At the same time, cattle stockmen used Montana's open range for grazing. In 1850, some stockmen started trading with travelers on the Oregon Trail. As the pioneers with their wagons and livestock trudged along the trail, the ranchers swapped one healthy cow for two worn-out ones. The stockmen would then fatten the cattle on rich Montana grass and drive them south to the Oregon Trail the following spring to begin the process again. More fresh livestock came with cowboys who drove herds of longhorn cattle up from Texas, from 1880 into the 1890s. Many ranchers became wealthy. It was cheap to buy cattle, it cost nothing to feed them, and shipping cattle to markets using the new railroads was easy. Cities along the rail lines, such as Miles City and Billings, became major livestock centers.

The open-range boom in the 1880s was due to several things. Demand for beef was high, with the increased numbers of city dwellers in the East. And with the coming of the railroads, transportation to the East was readily available. In addition, the confinement of American Indians to reservations and the shrinking bison herds opened up huge expanses of land.

Hunters pursued bison in the early 1880s for a variety of reasons. A new tanning method made it more profitable to sell the hides. Railroad companies encouraged people to kill bison. Thrill-seekers joined in the excitement of the hunt. Although millions of bison roamed the western plains in 1880, the bison was on the brink of extinction in 1884.

Ranchers in Montana drive cattle today much as they did in the 1880s.

Statehood

Boom times brought people—and wealth—to the Montana Territory. But many Montanans longed for statehood. Statehood would recognize Montana's importance to the country and provide full representation in Congress. The state could tax local corporations. And local citizens would be able to elect their own executive and judicial officials.

In 1889, U.S. president Benjamin Harrison signed a law that would give four states—including Montana—immediate statehood, after each one drafted a constitution. Montanans wrote such a constitution, which was approved on October 1, 1889. Then, on November 8, 1889, the president proclaimed Montana the forty-first state in the Union. The people of Montana were asked to vote for their new state capital. They chose Helena over Virginia City and Anaconda by a small margin.

When Copper Was King

Once the Montana gold rush was over, miners discovered silver, copper, lead, and other valuable minerals. Unlike gold, which was found in streambeds and mined by filtering out the metal with pans, silver and copper were contained in a hard rock called ore that had to be dug out of mountainsides. Copper and silver miners used heavy machinery to tunnel underground. Smelters, factories that break metal away from ore, were built in Anaconda and Great Falls.

People across the nation were demanding more copper because it was used to manufacture wires for popular new inventions such as the telephone and electric lighting. By 1887, Montana was the nation's largest copper and silver producer. Butte was called "the richest hill on earth."

Hard-rock mining was very expensive. As a result, three wealthy men and their companies soon controlled all the mining operations. William Clark, Marcus Daly, and Fritz Heinze were called the Copper Kings. They competed with each other for power by owning newspapers and influencing judges and members of Congress who made decisions affecting the state. But one by one, they sold their holdings to Standard Oil, a powerful corporation whose mining operations were called the Anaconda Company. People in Butte just called it The Company.

The miners who came to Butte to work for the Anaconda Company came from all over the world. Butte became an ethnic melting pot. Irish, Cornish (from a county in England called Cornwall), Italian, and Chinese miners, as well as African Americans who came to Montana from other parts of the United States, worked twenty-four hours a day in the dangerous underground mines and the noisy, gritty smelters. The mining company controlled almost all parts of the miners' economic lives—the stores where miners shopped, the homes where they lived, and the banks that kept their money.

Workers sometimes felt the company was taking advantage of them, so they formed labor unions. Labor unions are organizations of workers formed to improve pay and working conditions. During the early part of the twentieth century, the Anaconda Company and the labor unions often clashed in violent protests. Such conflicts were reported in newspapers and soon gained national attention.

Homesteading

Farmers had moved into Montana's mining towns during the boom years to feed the new workers. When the mines declined, some workers turned to farming. Yet it was not until the beginning of the twentieth century that farmers settled

RAILROAD COMPANY AS LANDHOLDER

In 1900, the Northern Pacific Railroad owned more than 13 million acres (5.3 million ha) of land in Montana, part of its vast land grant from the federal government. Over the next seventeen years, the railroad sold off much of this land to small farmers at prices of up to $8.56 per acre (0.4 ha). By 1917, the company owned less than 3 million acres (1.2 million ha)—and had made large profits from the land sales.

on eastern Montana's plains. In 1862, the federal government had passed the Homestead Act. This law promised 160 acres (65 ha) of land to any man or woman willing to pay a small filing fee and live and work on the land for at least five years. Homesteaders did not flock to Montana's remote plains until the Enlarged Homestead Act of 1909. This new act gave any head of a household 320 acres (130 ha) of land and lowered the number of years needed to "prove up" from five to three.

Since lumber in the early twentieth century was costly, most farmers built small wood shacks they hoped would survive an icy Montana winter.

The railroads were also eager for more settlers. They placed advertisements in newspapers throughout the East Coast and even in Europe. Some pioneers and immigrants were promised "free land." Others paid for their farmland. The railroads also offered cheap rail fares, some including freight and sleeping facilities.

At the beginning of the twentieth century, farmers came from crowded eastern states. They also came from more distant European lands, including Sweden, Germany, Poland, Yugoslavia, France, Italy, Spain, Ireland, and Great Britain.

Once the newcomers stepped off the train and filed for their land, they quickly had to find shelter and water. On the dry, treeless plain, this was not easy. They built small houses, put up fences around their fields, dug wells by hand, and hauled water in barrels. Cattle ranchers did not welcome the new settlers, and the two groups argued bitterly about fences and water.

Homesteaders were not happy to find the soil so rocky, but they stuck by their claims and discovered that wheat grew well. Within a few years of the beginning of the homestead boom, more than 3 million acres (1.2 million ha) of land were being farmed. Towns sprung up around the railroad lines, rains fell, and wheat harvests were plentiful.

Just as the gold rush boom had to end, so did the homestead boom. The United States entered World War I (1914–1918) in 1917, and the federal government asked Montana's farmers to plow as much land as they could for food during the war. To speed up production, banks loaned farmers money for new equipment.

At the same time that farmers started plowing more dirt, a drought hit. After several rainless years, the soil was so dry that it blew away in "black blizzards." Making things worse for farmers, swarms of grasshoppers covered fields and ate crops to the ground. Soon, farmers could not harvest enough wheat or repay their bank loans. Many lost their farms. By 1925, half of Montana's farmers had "gone bust," and more than half of the region's banks had gone out of business.

Hard Times, a New Deal, and War

The 1920s were prosperous years for most of the United States, but in Montana, these years were often filled with despair. Wheat farmers and cattle and sheep ranchers could barely make a profit. Droughts set off deadly forest and grass fires that blazed throughout the state. And when the price of copper dropped, the Anaconda Company began to shift its business to low-cost mines in Mexico and Chile, leaving many Montana miners out of work. Montana was the only state to decrease in population in the 1920s.

By 1929, the national economy crashed and the entire country was suffering from bank failures and high unemployment. As the 1930s began, people had less money, and they had less use for trains to transport goods. As a result, many of Montana's railway workers, coal miners, and loggers also lost their jobs. This grim period in U.S. history is known as the Great Depression.

Between 1933 and 1939, the thirty-second U.S. president, Franklin Roosevelt, created a series of government programs, known as the New Deal, designed to help residents in all states. New Deal programs included the Works Progress Administration (WPA), the Public Works Administration (PWA), and the Civilian Conservation Corps (CCC). The WPA employed people for a wide range of construction and creative projects. The PWA built large projects such as Montana's Fort Peck Dam. The CCC, nicknamed Roosevelt's Tree Army, hired unemployed men to fight forest fires, build forest fire lookout towers, replant trees, and do other useful tasks in forests and other wilderness areas.

By the end of the 1930s, the U.S. government was focusing more on World War II (1939–1945) than on projects at home. The United States entered the conflict in 1941 and fought through the end of the war. In 1942, as part of the war effort, the federal government built two air force bases in Montana—Malmstrom and Glasgow.

Nearly 40,000 Montanans left the state to join the armed forces. Another 50,000 left to work in West Coast factories, manufacturing products for the war effort. Those at home went back to work growing wheat, raising cattle, logging, and mining.

Montana Today

Montana citizens still live with ups and downs. The Anaconda Company closed its copper mines in Butte and smelters in Anaconda and Great Falls in the 1980s. The closings put thousands of people out of work. A new owner bought and updated operations, but many jobs were lost to machines and to newer forms of mining. Copper mining in Montana still exists, although on a diminished level.

The timber and farming industries have changed, too. Today, logging companies and lumber mills employ fewer workers than in past decades. Farmers and ranchers continue to be faced with low prices for their products as well as spells of dry weather that make farming for a living a challenge. Most farms in Montana survive today by growing a variety of crops and raising a mixture of livestock.

Coal miners are still at work at the Rosebud Mine near Colstrip in southeastern Montana. Strip-mining began here in 1969. This type of mining involves clearing away the land (and destroying the plant life)

Surface mining, including strip-mining, requires removing the soil and rock to expose the mineral deposits. This technique can devastate the land and its wildlife.

that covers a coal deposit. The Rosebud coal-mining operation now includes three active pits.

In 1989, Montana celebrated its statehood centennial. Three years later, as a result of the 1990 Census, Montana lost one of its two seats in the U.S. House of Representatives. This change reflected the slow growth of Montana's population in the 1980s, compared to other states. The 2010 Census found that the number of Montanans grew by 9.7 percent in the first decade of the twenty-first century—matching the nationwide percentage increase. By 2012, the population exceeded one million state residents.

Montana has also grown in other ways. Tourism has become a major source of income and jobs in the state. More Americans and people from foreign countries are appreciating the beauty of Montana's wilderness areas and national parks and the opportunities for outdoor recreation.

As in other states, the years after the nationwide economic downturn that began in late 2007 were hard on Montanans. Yet, despite the state's economic troubles, most Montanans do not want to live anywhere else. Newcomers—many of them technology workers—have come to the state to get away from crowded cities. Some former residents have returned because they appreciate the Treasure State's natural beauty and way of life.

★ **c. 5000** BCE Prehistoric people hunt bison and mammoths in the region.

★ **c. 1600** Shoshone and Blackfeet Indians live in what is now Montana.

★ **1743** François and Louis-Joseph Vérendrye claim land that includes today's Montana for France.

★ **1803** The United States purchases the Louisiana Territory, including present-day Montana, from France.

★ **1805–1806** American explorers Meriwether Lewis and William Clark visit the region during their expedition west.

★ **1841** Father Pierre-Jean de Smet sets up St. Mary's Mission in the Bitterroot Valley.

★ **1858** James and Granville Stuart find gold near Deer Lodge.

★ **1864** The Montana Territory, split off from the Idaho Territory, is formed.

★ **1876** Sioux and Northern Cheyenne Indians defeat troops led by U.S. cavalry officer George Armstrong Custer at the Battle of the Little Bighorn.

★ **1889** Montana becomes the forty-first U.S. state.

★ **1909** Congress passes the Enlarged Homestead Act, and a homesteading boom begins in eastern Montana.

★ **1916** Jeannette Rankin of Montana becomes the first woman elected to the U.S. Congress.

★ **1933** Construction of the Fort Peck Dam begins.

★ **1972** Montanans vote for a new state constitution.

★ **1989** Montana celebrates the 100th anniversary of its statehood.

★ **1995** Gray wolves, native to the area, are reintroduced into Yellowstone National Park.

★ **2000** Wildfires burn nearly 1 million acres (405,000 ha) in the Bitterroot Valley.

★ **2005** The Judith Gap Wind Farm opens, providing electricity for Montana and neighboring states.

★ **2012** The state's population exceeds one million, according to an estimate by the U.S. Census Bureau.

The People

Montanans are fiercely proud to be citizens of their state. Throughout Montana's history, people have come from around the world to settle in this remarkable state and call it home.

People and Places

According to the 2010 U.S. Census, almost one million people lived in Montana as of April 1 of that year. By 2012, the Census Bureau estimated that the state's population had passed one million. But because Montana is so large, it is far from crowded. Forty-six out of Montana's fifty-six counties are considered "frontier" counties because they have an average population of six or fewer people per square mile (2.6 sq km). Statewide, there are only seven persons living per square mile (2.6 sq km). Compared to other parts of the country, that is very few. New York City, for example, has more than 27,000 people per square mile (2.6 sq km).

> ## In Their Own Words
>
> *I was born in Hamilton, but my dad was in the military, so I grew up all over the globe. As soon as I could, I moved back here; nothing holds a candle to this place!*
>
> —A Bitterroot Valley resident

At guest ranches in Montana, ranch hands share their way of life with people from other parts of the world.

Billings was founded in 1877 as Coulson. It was renamed in 1882 after the Northern Pacific Railroad Company president Frederick H. Billings.

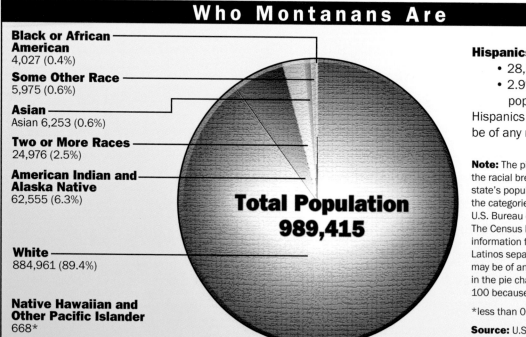

Who Montanans Are

Black or African American
4,027 (0.4%)

Some Other Race
5,975 (0.6%)

Asian
Asian 6,253 (0.6%)

Two or More Races
24,976 (2.5%)

American Indian and Alaska Native
62,555 (6.3%)

White
884,961 (89.4%)

Native Hawaiian and Other Pacific Islander
668*

Total Population 989,415

Hispanics or Latinos:
- 28,565 people
- 2.9% of the state's population

Hispanics or Latinos may be of any race.

Note: The pie chart shows the racial breakdown of the state's population based on the categories used by the U.S. Bureau of the Census. The Census Bureau reports information for Hispanics or Latinos separately, since they may be of any race. Percentages in the pie chart may not add to 100 because of rounding.

*less than 0.1%

Source: U.S. Bureau of the Census, 2010 Census

The Museum of the Rockies in Bozeman interprets the cultural history of Montana, Idaho, and Wyoming. Visitors can view American Indian artifacts, textiles and clothing, archaeological collections, tools, and vehicles.

Only slightly more than one-third of Montanans live in urban areas. The bigger cities and towns are rather small, compared to some other cities in the country. Billings has the highest population, with slightly more than 100,000 people. Missoula and Great Falls are next in size, with populations of around 70,000 and 60,000, respectively. The next largest cities are Bozeman, Butte, Helena, and Kalispell.

Montana's cities offer residents and visitors many lively events, including Butte's Heritage Festival or Missoula's First Night Missoula. The cities also offer unique museums, such as the Museum of the Rockies in Bozeman and the C. M. Russell Art Museum and the Lewis and Clark National Historic Trail Interpretive Center in Great Falls. The state also has historic parks, art galleries, theaters, and symphony orchestras.

Although Montanans prize their wide-open spaces and their solitude, many small towns, especially on the plains in eastern Montana, are shrinking. Young people from farm families move away to attend school or to find jobs. Throughout the plains, deserted homesteads and farms can be seen.

But other parts of the state have seen increasing populations. For the past few decades, newcomers have found their way to Montana, hoping to enjoy its special way of life. Most of them settle in the scenic, mountain-ringed valleys of western Montana, such as the Bitterroot, the Gallatin, and the Paradise valleys.

Diversity

American Indians were the first people to settle in Montana. Today, eleven tribal groups, each with its own language and culture, live on seven reservations in Montana. The Blackfeet tribe has the most members in Montana, numbering around 9,400. The Crow Reservation and the Fort Peck Indian Reservation, the homeland of Assiniboine and Sioux tribes, are the state's largest. Yet overall, American Indians make up only about 6 percent of the state's population.

Next to settle in Montana were miners and smelter workers who came from Ireland, Cornwall (in England), Scotland, Finland, Italy, Germany, Eastern Europe, and China, as well as the eastern United States. They settled in cities such as Butte, Anaconda, and Great Falls. To this day, these cities have rich ethnic neighborhoods full of traditional foods and celebrations. Cornish pasties are still considered a signature dish of Butte, for example.

Butte is also known for its large Irish-American population. In the mid-1800s, Irish immigrants were not welcomed by many East Coast communities. As a result, Irish workers moved out west to cities such as Butte for a chance to earn better wages and get a fresh start.

After the miners and factory workers moved to Montana, farmers and ranchers arrived. Many came from states farther east. Others were of Scandinavian, Russian, German, or English heritage. Overall, about 89 percent of Montana's residents today are white European-Americans.

Hispanic Americans make up almost 3 percent of the population. After the Civil War, African Americans moved to Montana to join in the mining boom, but once the boom ended, many left for better jobs elsewhere. Today, 0.4 percent of the population is African American. After the Vietnam War ended in the 1970s, many Southeast Asian immigrants moved to the state, mainly forming communities in the Bitterroot Valley. Asian Americans make up 0.6 percent of the current total population.

Cultural celebrations in Montana, such as this Crow gathering, encourage the state's American Indians to embrace their rich heritages.

A number of different religious faiths are practiced in Montana, a reflection of the state's ethnic diversity. Many Montanans are Roman Catholic, the most common faith of Irish and Italian immigrants in the nineteenth century. Many other Montanans follow the Lutheran faith, introduced by German and Scandinavian farm families. There are many followers of various other Protestant faiths, as well as members of the Church of Jesus Christ of Latter-day Saints— also called Mormons.

Some Montanans follow the Hutterite faith. More than a century ago, Hutterite farmers from Russia and Germany settled the plains and valleys of Montana. Today, there are thirty-nine Hutterite communities. Hutterite families live together on large farms and ranches, where they produce most of the state's pork and much of its eggs and milk. They share their property and income, and they dress similarly. Men wear black pants, hats, and jackets, and women wear long dresses, vests, and scarves. Although Hutterites use modern farm machinery, as part of keeping their faith, they avoid such worldly goods as cars and electronics products.

Charles M. Russell: Artist

Born near St. Louis, Missouri, in 1864, Charles Russell moved to Montana in 1880 and hoped to become a cowboy. He was never as good a cowboy as he was an artist. For the next forty-six years, Russell created more than 4,000 paintings and sculptures representing his vision of the West. He filled his log-cabin studio with American Indian clothing, pottery, and tools, cowboy gear, weapons, and other items to inspire him. Russell died in 1926. Today, museums, galleries, and lovers of the American West continue to collect his art.

Jeannette Rankin: U.S. Congresswoman

Jeannette Rankin was born near Missoula in 1880. Six years before the Nineteenth Amendment to the U.S. Constitution guaranteed women nationwide the right to vote, Rankin campaigned for women's voting rights in her home state and won. In 1916, she also won a seat in the U.S. House of Representatives, becoming the first woman elected to Congress. During her political career, she promoted women's rights, protested against war, and supported child protection laws. Rankin died in 1973.

Evel Knievel: Motorcycle Daredevil

Evel Knievel, born Robert Craig Knievel in Butte in 1938, was raised by his grandparents. Knievel began performing one-man motorcycle stunts in 1968. After jumping over the huge fountains of a Las Vegas, Nevada, hotel, he crashed and was in a coma for almost a month. Other stunts included jumping over 50 stacked cars in 1973 and fourteen buses in 1975. During his career, Knievel made more than 300 jumps and broke nearly forty bones in his body. He retired in 1980 and died in 2007 of natural causes.

Jack Horner: Paleontologist

Jack Horner is one of the most famous dinosaur researchers in the world. Born in Shelby in 1946, Horner began digging for fossils when he was a child. One of his most important finds was the fossilized eggs and nests of duck-billed dinosaurs. His discovery provided strong evidence that dinosaurs lived in family groups and watched over their young. In 2001, Horner and his team, on a dig in Montana's badlands, discovered bones of the largest *Tyrannosaurus rex* ever found. Horner is the curator of paleontology at the Museum of the Rockies at Montana State University in Bozeman.

Dana Carvey: Actor and Comedian

Dana Carvey, born in Missoula in 1955, started his entertainment career as a stand-up comedian. Carvey then spent seven seasons performing on the popular sketch-comedy TV show *Saturday Night Live*, where he created and portrayed many memorable characters. He is well-known for his comical impersonations of presidents, musicians, and other actors. Since leaving *Saturday Night Live*, Carvey has starred in several movies and has won awards for his work, including an Emmy in 1993.

Michelle Williams: Actress

Born in 1980 in Kalispell, Michelle Williams moved to southern California with her family when she was nine. She began acting as a teenager and landed her first big role at the age of sixteen, in the hit teen show *Dawson's Creek*. Williams received an Academy Award nomination for her supporting role in *Brokeback Mountain* (2005). She has been nominated for Best Actress for her performances in *Blue Valentine* (2010) and *My Week with Marilyn* (2011).

INDIAN EDUCATION FOR ALL

In 2005, the Montana legislature provided funding for public schools to teach all Montana schoolchildren about their state's American Indian cultures. The focus on various tribes has helped American Indian students feel proud of their distinct and rich heritage.

Education

Education is very important to Montanans. Taxpayers do their best to provide a good education to all students, whether they live in a city or in a rural area. Schools in small towns are important hubs for community activities, from youth sports such as basketball and football to public meetings or cultural events such as concerts and plays.

Montana has two large public university systems—Montana State University and the University of Montana. Montana State University has campuses in Billings, Bozeman, and Havre, as well as the College of Technology in Great Falls. The University of Montana's main campus is in Missoula. Three additional campuses are located in Butte, Helena, and Dillon. Students can also attend various community colleges. Montana offers three private institutions of higher learning. They are Carroll College in Helena, the University of Great Falls, and Rocky Mountain College in Billings.

Each American Indian reservation has a college, run by the tribes. Dr. Joe

The University of Montana at Missoula has more than 10,000 undergraduate students. Popular majors include business, communications, and natural resources and conservation.

McDonald helped create Salish Kootenai College on the Flathead Reservation and served as its president for three decades. He is also the founder of the nationwide American Indian College Fund, which raises money for American Indian students. "Family is all important to us, and we try to match the school to the community—kind of like a spider on a mirror. Arts, music, and the lore of the Crow Nation are at the heart of our program," said Dr. Janine Pease, former president of the Little Big Horn College on the Crow Reservation.

Sports in Montana

Montana has no major league sports teams. Four Montana teams play minor-league baseball in the Pioneer League. The state's minor league baseball fans support the Billings Mustangs, the Great Falls Voyagers, the Helena Brewers, and the Missoula Osprey.

In college sports, both the University of Montana Grizzlies and the Montana State University Bobcats compete in the Big Sky Conference. The University of Montana offers fourteen intercollegiate men's and women's sports programs. Montana State University has thirteen programs, including men's and women's ski, tennis, basketball, and cross-country teams.

The Billings Mustangs have been affiliated with Major League Baseball's Cincinnati Reds since 1974.

A skier launches off a ridge at Big Sky ski area in front of Lone Mountain.

Living in and Visiting Montana

Montana is the place to be if you love the outdoors. The state has many streams for fishing, rivers for rafting, and wilderness areas for hiking, horseback riding, rock climbing, and hunting. Residents and tourists like to swim, boat, and visit the state's national parks. A favorite event in July is the Governor's Cup Walleye Tournament, in which fishers from all over the West compete for the biggest walleye in Fort Peck Lake. In the winter, there is powdery snow for skiing, snowboarding, and snowmobiling. Ski slopes and backcountry trails are full of Montanans and others enjoying a winter's day.

The Chippewa-Cree Rocky Boy Powwow offers dance, costume, and drumming competitions, as well as traditional food, exhibits, and crafts.

Around the state, there are festivals of all kinds, honoring ethnic heritage, Western history, and religious holidays. Each year, the Chippewa and Cree tribes host the Rocky Boy Powwow. The event celebrates American Indian heritage and culture. In August, the Crow Fair is an annual gathering open to the public, and many say that the fair has the largest gathering of tepees anywhere.

The town of Libby celebrates its logging past with food and entertainment during Libby Logger Days. The German harvest celebration Oktoberfest fills the streets of Anaconda each year with traditional dance, music, and food. Billings honors Mexican-American culture in an Annual Mexican Fiesta in July.

There are other ways Montanans show their uniqueness. There are kayak races, battlefield re-enactments, rodeos, and more. One special event is the Festival of Nations, held in the former mining town of Red Lodge, where the community pays tribute to the people who first settled the area. Visitors enjoy ethnic foods, foreign movies, Irish fiddlers, Italian and American Indian dancers, Scandinavian children's dancers, Slavic pig roasts, and a parade honoring people of all nations. This community event shows the close-knit spirit of Montanans.

★ Race to the Sky

For six days every February since 1986, dozens of men and women mushers and their dogs compete in this spectacular sled-dog race through parts of the Rocky Mountains. Winners of the 350-mile (550-km) competition have gone on to win the famous Iditarod sled-dog race across Alaska.

★ St. Patrick's Day Celebration

Called the Best St. Patrick's Day Party in the West, this celebration brings crowds dressed in green to the streets of Butte every March 17. To celebrate Ireland's patron saint, there are Irish dancers, musicians, actors, a festive parade, and a foot race.

★ Custer's Last Stand Re-enactment and Little Big Horn Days

At the end of June, hundreds of re-enactors gather near the site of the Battle of the Little Bighorn to relive the event sometimes called Custer's Last Stand. The re-enactment is part of the four-day festival Little Big Horn Days, held in Hardin. Included are art exhibits, a quilt show, a Grand Ball, living-history exhibits, and traditional Crow Indian food.

★ Lewis and Clark Days Festival

Two historic sites on Lewis and Clark's route are located near Cut Bank—Camp Disappointment and the Two Medicine Fight Site. Cut Bank citizens hold a festival every July to honor the explorers and their party. The festival includes a parade, a chili cook-off, a crafts fair, concerts, and tours of parts of Lewis and Clark's trail.

★ North American Indian Days Celebration

Montana's largest tribe, the Blackfeet, hosts a celebration and powwow in July on the Blackfeet Reservation fairgrounds in Browning. For four days, visitors enjoy traditional costumes and dress, American Indian dance and drumming competitions, stick games, food, rodeos, and races.

★ Montana State Fair

In late July and early August, Montanans pour into the Montana Expo Park near Great Falls to celebrate their shared culture and history. There are carnival rides, livestock shows, horse races, lumberjack contests, arts and crafts, food, and fun.

★ "Running of the Sheep" Sheep Drive

In September, at the "Running of the Sheep" Sheep Drive, hundreds of sheep charge down Reed Point's Main Street to the delight of spectators. A parade and dance add more fun to the event.

★ Yellowstone River Boat Float

Buckle up your life jacket and launch your boat in the beautiful Yellowstone River. People from all over the country gather on the second weekend in July each year to spend three lazy, sunny days floating on the Yellowstone from Livingston to Columbus. The float retraces part of the route of the Lewis and Clark Expedition.

★ Montana Folk Festival

Every year in July, the three-day Montana Folk Festival is held in Butte, against the backdrop of this historic town. The finest traditional musicians from Montana and around the country perform on multiple stages.

★ Annual Bison Roundup

The National Bison Range Wildlife Refuge in Moiese is home to 350 to 500 bison. In October, visitors can watch the rangers on horseback herd the snorting, stampeding bison into sturdy corrals. After checking on the health of the bison, the rangers auction some of them to ranchers and donate others to tribal herds.

How the
Government Works

From the time that Lewis and Clark explored the West until the years before Montana became a territory in 1864, many of the region's trappers, miners, and adventurers had little use for an orderly government. But as more people arrived, an organized set of rules was needed. In 1864, citizen lawmakers gathered to write more than seven hundred pages of laws for the new Montana Territory. Twenty-five years later, lawmakers drafted a state constitution, and Montana became the forty-first state on November 8, 1889.

Powerful business leaders influenced many rules written into the first constitution and laws passed in the early years of statehood. Soon, however, citizens began to demand changes, or amendments, to their constitution and new laws. Montanans gave women the right to vote in 1914. They also passed laws that protected workers and children, and it was one of the first states to adopt the lawmaking methods of initiative and referendum. In an initiative, citizens can suggest a law, and if enough people vote in favor of the proposal in an election, then it becomes a law without having to be approved by the state legislature. In a referendum, citizens can vote to have an existing law changed or removed.

By the late 1960s, Montanans had added forty-one amendments to their constitution. Voters decided that was too many and asked lawmakers to write a new constitution. Ratified in 1972, the new constitution has some of the

The Montana state capitol, located in Helena, opened on July 4, 1902.

TRIBAL GOVERNMENTS

Each of the seven American Indian reservations in Montana has its own government. This government manages schools, businesses, and natural resources on the reservation. Residents of each reservation elect a council and a chairperson to head the government. The reservation governments collect their own taxes and run their own police and court systems.

most progressive provisions in the nation. Citizens are guaranteed rights to individual privacy and open meetings. The constitution also affirms a right to clean air and water. Montana's 1972 constitution was the first state constitution that recognizes and promises to preserve the "unique cultural heritage of the American Indians."

From Local to State

Montana's fifty-six counties are made up of cities and towns. Nearly every city or town in Montana has its own local government. The cities or towns may be run by a manager, a mayor, selectmen, or a town or city council. These governmental bodies manage local budgets, local public schools, land use, and other zoning concerns.

The state is divided into districts. These districts have elected officials who represent them in the state government. Redistricting takes place every ten years to ensure that all districts have populations of similar size.

The state government passes laws and adopts policies on issues that affect the whole state. State government concerns include setting statewide education policies, maintaining law and order, providing emergency services, and overseeing basic services such as transportation, communication, and water. The

Branches of Government

EXECUTIVE ★ ★ ★ ★ ★ ★ ★ ★ ★

The chief officer of the executive branch is the governor. He or she is elected to a four-year term. Generally, a person may not serve as governor for more than eight years in any sixteen-year period. But an official can be reelected by a write-in vote, even if he or she has already served eight years. The lieutenant governor, secretary of state, attorney general, auditor, and superintendent of public schools are other key members of the executive branch. Like the governor, they serve four-year terms. The governor's duties include proposing new laws and appointing important officials. He or she must also sign bills into law or reject (veto) them.

LEGISLATIVE ★ ★ ★ ★ ★ ★ ★ ★

The Montana legislature has two chambers, the senate and the house of representatives. The senate is made up of 50 state senators, and the house has 100 state representatives. Senators hold office for four years, and elections take place for half of the senate every two years. Representatives hold office for two years. An individual may serve in either chamber for eight years of any sixteen-year period. Members of the legislature meet every other year for ninety days, unless a special session is called.

JUDICIAL ★ ★ ★ ★ ★ ★ ★ ★ ★

The judicial branch is a system of courts made up of a supreme court, district courts, and lower courts. The supreme court is the highest court in the state and oversees all other courts. Decisions of lower courts can be appealed to the supreme court, which can approve or change them. The supreme court can also rule on whether a state law agrees with or violates the state constitution. The supreme court has a chief justice and six associate justices. They are elected to eight-year terms. District courts are trial courts. District judges are elected to six-year terms. Lower courts such as city courts and justices of the peace rule on small claims and traffic violations. There are also a water court and a workers' compensation court.

state government has three branches—executive, legislative, and judicial. The state of Montana is represented at the federal level by two U.S. senators and one representative in the U.S. House of Representatives.

MANSFIELD OF MONTANA

Born in 1903 to Irish immigrant parents in New York City, Mike Mansfield moved to Montana as a child. At age fourteen, he lied about his age to join the U.S. Navy and fight in World War I. After the war, Mansfield worked in a Montana copper mine. Beginning in 1943, he served five terms in the U.S. House of Representatives. Starting in 1953, he served four terms in the U.S. Senate, and he held the powerful position of Senate majority leader from 1961 to 1977. Mansfield was majority leader longer than anyone else in Senate history. In 1977, President Jimmy Carter appointed him the U.S. ambassador to Japan. Mansfield died in 2001 at the age of ninety-eight. He is buried in Arlington National Cemetery in Virginia.

How a Bill Becomes a Law

Although voters can create new laws through the initiative process, most new laws are created by the state legislature. A proposed law, or bill, can often begin in either the senate or the house of representatives (except that bills involving spending money from the state budget must originate in the house). Only a member of the legislature can introduce a bill.

A legislator who has an idea for a bill asks the legislative staff to write a draft of the bill. The bill is read to the chamber that legislator is a member of (either the senate or the house). Then, it is sent to the appropriate committee of that chamber for consideration. A bill having to do with farming, for example, is sent to the Agriculture Committee. Every legislator serves on at least one committee.

The relevant committee holds a public hearing for citizens to share their views about the bill. The committee then votes to approve the bill—as is or with changes—or to reject it. A rejected bill goes no further, or "dies" in committee.

Sometimes a committee will table a bill, or take no action on it. A tabled bill also usually dies in committee.

A bill approved in committee goes back to the entire chamber in which it originated for a second reading. During this reading, the bill is debated and possibly amended, and members vote on it. If passed, the bill moves to a third reading, and another vote is taken. If the bill passes by a majority vote after the third reading, it is sent to the other chamber of the legislature. There, it goes through the same process of committee and perhaps full-chamber consideration. Sometimes, the second chamber makes changes to a bill before passing it. If the two chambers have passed different versions of a bill, often a conference committee, with members from both chambers, is appointed to find a compromise between the house and senate versions. This compromise then has to be approved by both the house and the senate.

A bill that passes in both chambers in the same form goes to the governor. The governor can sign the bill into law, veto the bill, or take no action. If the governor takes no action, the bill becomes law in ten days. If the governor vetoes a bill, such a bill often does not become law. However, the legislature can override the veto. If both chambers again vote in favor of the bill—by a two-thirds majority in each chamber—the bill becomes law despite the governor's disapproval.

Contacting Lawmakers

★ ★ ★ ★ ★ ★ ★ ★ ★ ★ ★ ★

If you are interested in contacting Montana's state legislators, go to

http://leg.mt.gov/css/find a legislator.asp

You can search for legislators and their contact information by name, zip code, or district.

Montana's lawmakers meet in the state capitol in Helena.

Making a Living

"Everything comes from the land, water, sun, or air," said Montana historian Joseph Kinsey Howard. "They are natural elements owned in common by all and not worth anything in terms of money. If everything is made of land, air, water, and sun, where does it get its value? From labor." Making a living in Montana has never been easy. Citizens have often had to rebuild after a drought, a storm, or a fire and start all over again. Throughout their history, Montanans have proudly worked with—and against—the elements.

Farming and Ranching

Agriculture is the backbone of Montana's economy. Of the more than 29,000 farms and ranches in the state, most are family-run. A farm typically grows crops, and a ranch raises livestock. Farms and ranches that do both tend to be the most successful. The plains region of north-central Montana known as the Golden Triangle has rich, black soil and produces the state's best wheat and barley. Ranches raise cattle, hogs, sheep, llamas, and horses. Together, cattle and wheat make up about 70 percent of the state's total income from agriculture. This brings

Quick Facts

OUTNUMBERED
Montana has about 2,500,000 head of cattle. That means the state has about two and a half times as many cows, bulls, and steers as it has residents.

Farms in Montana produce many crops, including wheat, barley, lentils, potatoes, corn, hay, canola, and sugar beets.

Workers & Industries

Industry	Number of People Working in That Industry	Percentage of All Workers Who Are Working in That Industry
Education and health care	110,281	23.6%
Wholesale and retail businesses	67,450	14.4%
Publishing, media, entertainment, hotels, and restaurants	58,777	12.5%
Construction	37,818	8.1%
Professionals, scientists, and managers	37,760	8.1%
Farming, fishing, forestry, and mining	33,141	7.1%
Government	30,320	6.5%
Banking and finance, insurance, and real estate	26,254	5.6%
Transportation and public utilities	24,503	5.2%
Manufacturing	20,699	4.4%
Other Services	20,671	4.4%
Totals	**467,674**	**100%**

Notes: Figures above do not include people in the armed forces.
"Professionals" includes people such as doctors and lawyers.

Source: U.S. Bureau of the Census, 2010 estimates

Most cattle ranchers in Montana operate cow-calf ranches. On these ranches, the calves graze in herds near their mothers.

Montana more than $2 billion dollars each year.

Nearly 61 million acres (25 million ha) of land is used for farms or ranches, and Montana ranks second in the nation in the amount of agricultural land. The average size of a farm or ranch in Montana is a little more than 2,000 acres (800 ha). Ranches, especially in eastern counties, are generally larger, in order to provide enough grazing land for their animals. Farms are somewhat smaller.

In some western valleys, the number of farms is decreasing. Newcomers who move to the area to retire or to escape busier lifestyles are looking for scenic farmland on which to build their houses. During hard times, farmers see this as a way to make money. They divide their big farms into 20- to 40-acre (8- to 16-ha) plots of land, called ranchettes, and sell off the plots. Periods of drought or low prices make it increasingly hard for farmers to pay their bills. As farms are broken up and sold, many citizens worry about losing an important part of their state's history and culture.

A farmer feeds sheep on his ranch near Hilger.

RECIPE FOR HUCKLEBERRY FOOL

In Montana, berries grow in the wild and on farms. Many Montanans love wild mountain huckleberries. But if you cannot find huckleberries, you can make a berry fool with any juicy berries. (You may want to strain berries with lots of seeds, such as raspberries or strawberries.)

WHAT YOU NEED

- 2 cups (500 milliliters) fresh huckleberries (or other juicy berries)
- $1\frac{1}{2}$ cups (360 ml) heavy whipping cream
- 3 tablespoons (20 grams) powdered sugar
- $\frac{1}{4}$ teaspoon (1 ml) vanilla extract

Carefully wash the berries, drain the water, and remove any stems or leaves from the berries. Set aside twelve whole berries. Place the rest in a large bowl and mash them until they are a lumpy liquid.

Pour the heavy whipping cream into a new bowl, and use an electric mixer to beat it. (You can ask an adult for help with the mixer.) Mix the cream until it starts to thicken. Add the sugar and the vanilla, and mix until the cream forms stiff peaks.

Slowly pour the crushed berries into the whipped cream, and gently stir using a rubber spatula. The berries should make swirls of color in the cream. Scoop the fool into glass cups or bowls. Using the twelve whole berries that you set aside, place two berries on top of each serving and refrigerate for 3 hours. You may want to serve your huckleberry fool with a cookie or slice of cake.

Mining

Gold was the first important mineral found in the rich hills and valleys of the state. Silver and copper were discovered later. Today, gold, silver, and copper are still mined, but not as much as they once were. A Stillwater County mine is an industry leader. It mines gold, silver, lead, and zinc, along with the more rare metals platinum and palladium. Platinum and palladium are used in jewelry, dentistry, pharmaceutical drugs, chemical products, and electronics. Montana is one of the major producers of talc in the United States. Other minerals mined in the state include sand and gravel.

Present-day mining techniques use machinery, which means fewer jobs for workers. But in the old mining towns of Anaconda and Butte, there is some job growth. The Anaconda smelter site and the abandoned open-pit mines near Butte have left behind hazardous wastes. One serious situation is the Berkeley Pit above

The Stillwater Mining Company in Montana is the primary producer of platinum and palladium in the United States. These rare metals have many practical uses.

The Berkeley Pit, started in 1955, was a large open-pit copper mine. Its operations ceased in 1982.

the town of Butte. This polluted hole is filled with water that could spill over into nearby streams and drinking water sources. Scientists and other skilled workers have built water treatment plants and other facilities to help protect the city and the environment from this danger. Efforts to clean up the Berkeley Pit have created jobs for many people in Butte.

Montana also contains deposits of minerals used for fuel, such as coal, petroleum, and natural gas. Settlers first used coal for heating, and later, the railroads used it to power trains. Today, near the town of Colstrip, huge mining operations pull coal from the ground and use it to fuel four large, coal-burning electrical generators. The electricity is sold to other states. Coal-fired power plants are also located in Billings. Oil and natural gas are produced from rich deposits in the plains of eastern Montana. Underground pipelines carry the oil and gas to refineries. (Another resource of Montana's open plains is wind. In recent years, wind turbines have been set up to convert the power of wind into electricity.)

Forest Products

Forests cover nearly one quarter of Montana—about 22.5 million acres (9 million ha). The timber industry, or the business of cutting trees and preparing them for use, started in the early days of white settlement. Today, most of the state's forest products are shipped out of state for use in building homes and furniture. Wood from Montana's forests is also processed into paper, plywood, construction materials, and telephone poles. In 2010, the total sales value of Montana's wood and paper products was an estimated $325 million. This is significantly lower than 2005, when sales were just under $1.2 billion. The 2008 collapse of the home-building industry nationwide contributed to this decrease in sales.

The timber industry is also hurt by forest fires in Montana. In 2000, nearly 600,000 acres (240,000 ha) of forest burned in the state. Fires began in June and continued through mid-September. Nearly half of the acreage burned was in the Bitterroot National Forest. A Bitterroot Valley resident said, "It was awful. We watched elk come out of the hills, and they were steaming!" The fire brought communities together to talk about the best way to combat forest fires in the future.

Manufacturing

Manufacturing is one of the smaller industries in Montana. Meatpacking, flour milling, and sugar refining are the state's major food-processing operations. The manufacture of plywood and paper products is part of the timber industry. There are petroleum refineries in Billings, Great Falls, and Laurel. An aluminum plant is located in Columbia Falls.

Wheat

There are many kinds of wheat, such as hard wheat, soft wheat, and durum. Durum wheat is used to make pasta. Montana's farmers produce hard wheat and durum. The state is third among the top wheat-producing states in the country.

Sheep

Farmers first brought sheep to Montana during the mining boom. But the miners preferred eating beef over mutton (meat from sheep). As a result, sheep farmers sold wool to be used as mattress stuffing. The sheep industry is much smaller than the cattle industry, but sheep ranchers in Montana today harvest more than 2 million pounds (900,000 kg) of good-quality long-haired wool from their flocks each year.

Handcrafted Log Homes

Montana is a leading producer of log homes. These energy-efficient homes are made from Western red cedar or pine. Instead of logging forests for their materials, many builders are able to use dead or burned trees. Most of the log homes are delivered to buyers in other states or countries.

Coal

Montana is the fifth-largest producer of coal in the United States. Nearly 45 million tons (40 million metric tons) are mined each year. Most of the mines are strip mines located on federal or tribal lands. The coal is used to generate electricity that is sold to states in the Midwest and the West.

Missiles

Located at the eastern edge of Great Falls, the Malmstrom Air Force Base encompasses 3,500 acres (1,400 ha). It is the command center for 150 Minuteman III intercontinental ballistic missiles. Military technicians and specialists test and care for these missiles as part of the nation's military defense.

Tourism

Tourism is the state's fastest-growing industry. State residents and millions of visitors each year spend more than $2 billion at attractions such as historic sites, trout-fishing streams, national parks, ski slopes, and guest ranches. Tourism and recreation businesses support more than 34,000 jobs in Montana.

Hikers in Montana follow a trail in Glacier National Park.

At Your Service

Service jobs, such as jobs in health care, are the fastest-growing part of Montana's economy. Colleges and universities provide education, research, and clerical jobs. There are also employment opportunities in government, transportation, publishing, and printing. Other service jobs are in banking, insurance, law enforcement, social services, retail sales, and tourism.

The tourism industry produces the second-highest amount of income for the state, after agriculture. Montana tourism brought in more than $2.4 billion in 2010. People come to Montana to enjoy the great outdoors. More than 10 million tourists visit its ski resorts, guest ranches, remarkable national parks, and other unique attractions each year. There are many ways to appreciate the Treasure State.

The Montana state flag was adopted in 1905 and revised in 1981 and 1985. Large gold letters spell out Montana at the top of the dark blue flag. Below the letters is the state seal, displaying symbols of the state economy and landscape.

Montana's state seal, officially adopted in 1865, was revised in 1893 after Montana became a state. It shows the words The Great Seal of the State of Montana in a circle on a brown field. Inside the circle are tools symbolizing Montana's mining and farming economy—a plow, shovel, and pick. A landscape of mountains, the sun, and the Great Falls of the Missouri River form the background behind the tools. At the bottom is the state motto, Oro y Plata, which is Spanish for "gold and silver."

MONTANA

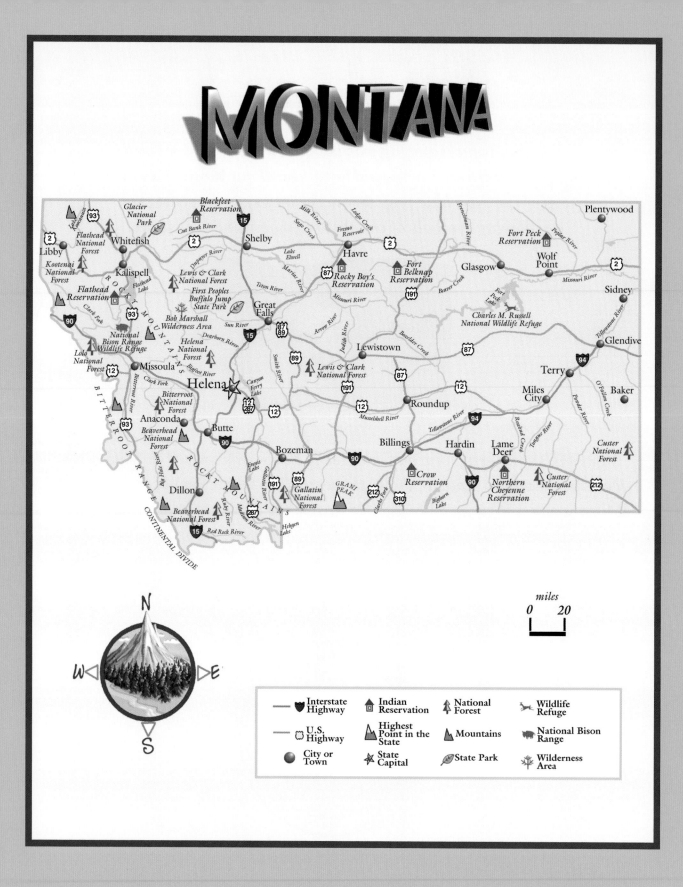

Glacier National Park
Blackfeet Reservation
Plentywood
Libby
Flathead National Forest
Whitefish
Kootenai National Forest
Kalispell
Shelby
Havre
Glasgow
Wolf Point
Sidney
Lewis & Clark National Forest
Fort Peck Reservation
Rocky Boy's Reservation
Fort Belknap Reservation
First Peoples Buffalo Jump State Park
Flathead Reservation
Bob Marshall Wilderness Area
Great Falls
Charles M. Russell National Wildlife Refuge
Glendive
National Bison Range Wildlife Refuge
Helena National Forest
Lewistown
Terry
Lolo National Forest
Missoula
Lewis & Clark National Forest
Roundup
Miles City
Baker
Helena
Bitterroot National Forest
Anaconda
Butte
Bozeman
Billings
Hardin
Lame Deer
Custer National Forest
Beaverhead National Forest
Crow Reservation
Northern Cheyenne Reservation
Dillon
Gallatin National Forest
GRANITE PEAK
Beaverhead National Forest

ROCKY MOUNTAINS
BITTERROOT RANGE
CONTINENTAL DIVIDE

miles
0   20

Legend:
- Interstate Highway
- U.S. Highway
- City or Town
- Indian Reservation
- Highest Point in the State
- State Capital
- National Forest
- Mountains
- State Park
- Wildlife Refuge
- National Bison Range
- Wilderness Area

Montana

words by Charles Cohan and music by Joseph Howard

Tell me of that Trea - sure State, Stor - y al - ways new, _____

Tell of its beau - ties grand And its hearts so true. _____

Moun - tains of sun - set fire, The land I love the best. _____

Let me grasp the hand of one From out the Gold - en West. _____

Mon - tan - a, Mon - tan - a, Glo - ry of the West. _____ Of

all the states from coast to coast You're eas - i - ly the best. _____ Mon -

tan - a, Mon - tan - a, Where skies are al - ways blue. _____

M - O - N - T - A - N - A, Mon-tan-a, ___ I love you. _____

BOOKS

Glynn, Gary. *Historic Photos of Montana*. Nashville, TN: Turner, 2009.

Josephson, Judith Pinkerton. *Who Was Sitting Bull?: And Other Questions about the Battle of Little Bighorn* (Six Questions of American History). Minneapolis, MN: Lerner, 2011.

Medicine Crow, Joseph. *Counting Coup: Becoming a Crow Chief on the Reservation and Beyond*. Des Moines, IA: National Geographic Children's Books, 2006.

Naden, Corinne J. *Jeannette Rankin* (Leading Women). New York: Benchmark Books, 2012.

Oberbillig, Deborah Richie. *Bird Feats of Montana: Including Yellowstone and Glacier National Parks*. Helena, MT: Farcountry Press, 2009.

Smith, Roland. *The Captain's Dog: My Journey with the Lewis and Clark Tribe*. San Anselmo, CA: Sandpiper, 2008.

WEBSITES

Montana Kids.com:
http://montanakids.com

Montana's Official State Travel Site:
http://www.visitmt.com/Experiences

Montana's Official State Website:
http://mt.gov

Ruth Bjorklund lives on Bainbridge Island, a ferry ride away from Seattle, Washington, with her husband, two children, two dogs, and four cats. She and her family believe there's no better place for a snowball fight than in Montana.

Ellen H. Todras is a freelance writer and editor. She has written parts of many social studies textbooks. She also has authored *Angelina Grimké: Voice of Abolition*, a young-adult biography, and other books about the United States. She loves history and enjoys bringing it to life for young people. She lives with her husband in Eugene, Oregon.

Page numbers in **boldface** are illustrations.